Absurdity
The Narrow Road

By

Joaquin E. Pavón

Absurdity: The Narrow Road

© 2026 Joaquin Enrique Pavón

Published by Pavón Press

All rights reserved.

No part of this book may be reproduced, stored in a retrieval system, or transmitted in any form or by any means electronic, mechanical, photocopying, recording, or otherwise without prior written permission from the author, except for brief quotations in reviews or scholarly works.

This is a work of nonfiction. Events, teachings, and reflections are presented from the author's perspective and experience.

Printed in the United States of America.

ISBN: 979-8-9948314-0-3

First Edition

PROLOGUE

INVOCATION: THE CRY OF A MAN BEING REMADE

I didn't start this journey with clarity. I started it with confusion, the kind that sits in your chest like fog, thick enough to breathe but too heavy to ignore. The world around me felt distorted, the people I trusted felt distant, and even the man I thought I was supposed to be felt like a stranger. I wasn't walking through life so much as feeling my way through it, hoping something solid would finally meet my hands.

But even in the confusion, something in me kept reaching upward. I didn't have the words for it then. I didn't have the discipline, the theology, or the understanding. What I had was a longing, a quiet ache for something higher, something clean, something true. I didn't know it yet, but that longing was the Spirit beginning His work in me, shaping me long before I had the sense to surrender.

Perfect submission wasn't even on my radar. I wasn't the type to bow easily. I wasn't the type to trust quickly. I wasn't the type to hand over control. But God doesn't wait for perfect men to begin perfecting them. He starts with the broken, the confused, the stubborn, the ones who don't even know they're being pursued.

And I was being pursued.

I felt it most when I prayed. Even when my prayers were clumsy, even when they were short, even when they were half-hearted, something shifted in me. I drew closer to Him without even trying. It was like stepping into a room where the air was different, calmer, cleaner, steadier. Prayer didn't fix everything around me, but it steadied everything inside me.

Life didn't get easier. If anything, the turbulence increased. Trials came in waves, and some days it felt like the ground beneath me was shaking. But even then, I wasn't undone. I wasn't destroyed. I wasn't abandoned. I stayed steady because He was steady. I stayed upright because He held me upright. I survived because He was there.

Strength isn't the absence of struggle. Strength is the presence of God in the middle of it.

I didn't know that at first. I had to learn it the hard way, through locked doors, dead ends, and moments where I had nowhere else to turn. But every time I reached the end of myself, I found Him waiting. Not with condemnation. Not with disappointment. But with the quiet, unshakeable presence of someone who had already decided not to let me go.

This chapter isn't about victory. It's about awakening. It's about the moment a man realizes he's being remade, not by force, not by fear, but by love that refuses to leave him where it found him.

This is where my story begins: in confusion, in longing, in prayer, in turbulence, in the slow, steady work of a God who knew me long before I knew myself.

PART I — TESTIMONY: THE MAN GOD PULLED OUT

Chapter 1

The Narrow Gate

I didn't know I was walking toward a gate. I didn't know there was a gate. All I knew was that my life had become a long hallway of noise, a hallway lined with mirrors that showed me versions of myself I didn't want to be, but kept becoming anyway.

The narrow gate isn't something you stumble into. It's something you collide with when the wide road finally collapses under its own weight.

For years, I lived inside the illusion that I could outrun consequence. That I could outthink conviction. That I could outmaneuver God.

But the truth is simple: No one outruns the One who made their feet.

The narrow gate is not attractive. It's not glamorous. It doesn't flatter your ego or applaud your independence. It confronts you. It exposes you. It strips you down to the truth you've been avoiding.

And for me, that truth was this:

I was lost. Not metaphorically. Not poetically. Actually lost.

Lost in pride. Lost in self deception. Lost in the belief that I could build my own meaning out of the scraps of my own desires.

The narrow gate appeared the moment I finally admitted that the wide road, the road of self-rule, self-gratification, self-worship had led me nowhere but deeper into myself.

And the deeper I went, the darker it became.

The narrow gate is not a doorway you walk through casually. It's a surrender. A yielding. A confession that the life you built on your own terms is not a life at all, just a performance with no audience and no ending.

When I reached that gate, I didn't walk through it with confidence. I crawled. I limped. I arrived bruised by my own decisions, humbled by my own failures, and exhausted by the weight of pretending I was fine.

But the gate didn't ask for perfection. It asked for honesty.

And honesty was the first thing I had run out of.

The narrow gate is not narrow because God is cruel. It's narrow because truth is narrow. Because life is narrow. Because the way home is not found in a thousand directions, only one.

And I had finally reached the point where I was willing to stop running from it.

Chapter 2

Testimony In Fragments: The Man I Was

I didn't become who I am by accident. I lived through years where my life felt like a collection of broken pieces, sharp edges, scattered memories, and choices I didn't fully understand until much later. I didn't grow up with a blueprint for righteousness. I learned most of my lessons the hard way, through the wrong people, the wrong environments, and the wrong impulses that felt right in the moment.

I learned more than I ever wanted from bad company. People say you become who you surround yourself with, and I used to laugh at that. I thought I was immune, like I could walk through fire and come out without the smell of smoke. But the truth is, the people around me shaped me in ways I didn't see until I was older. Their habits became my habits. Their logic became my logic. Their chaos became my normal.

I became a walking target without even realizing it. Not because I was tough, or dangerous, or feared, but because I was lost. When you're lost, you drift into places where lost people gather. You start living in rooms where everyone is trying to rebuild themselves, one meeting at a time, one confession at a time, one relapse at a time. I saw people break and try to put themselves back together with nothing but willpower and desperation. I didn't know it then, but I was one of them.

Some habits pretend to sleep. They don't die. They don't disappear. They just wait. They lie still long enough for you to think you're free, and then they rise the moment you let your guard down. I carried habits like that, quiet addictions, quiet escapes, quiet compromises. They didn't roar; they whispered. And whispers are sometimes more dangerous than screams.

But not everything deserves another chance. I had to learn that mercy doesn't mean returning to what broke you. Forgiveness doesn't mean reopening the door. Some things need to stay dead. Some habits need to stay buried. Some environments need to stay behind you like a city you escaped from in the middle of the night.

There were moments when I felt like I was rebuilding myself with my bare hands. Moments when I sat in silence, staring at the pieces of my life, wondering how I ended up there. Moments when I felt like I was watching myself from the outside, a man drifting, a man searching, a man pretending he had control when he didn't.

But even in those moments, something in me refused to give up. I didn't know it was God at the time. I didn't know He was the one keeping me from falling off the edge completely. I didn't know He was the one whispering to me in the middle of the noise, telling me there was more, telling me I wasn't finished, telling me I wasn't beyond repair.

Looking back, I see it clearly. He was there in the rooms where people tried to rebuild themselves. He was there in the friendships that fell apart. He was there in the habits that tried to reclaim me. He was there in the moments when I felt like a ghost in my own life.

This chapter of my life wasn't pretty. It wasn't holy. It wasn't admirable. But it was real. And it was necessary.

Because before God rebuilds a man, He lets him see the ruins. Before He restores, He reveals. Before He heals, He exposes the wound.

I was a man in fragments, but even fragments can become a foundation when God decides to build.

Chapter 3

The Wilderness Within

The wilderness is not a location. It is a condition of the soul.

You don't have to be surrounded by sand to feel lost. You don't need to be in a desert to feel dry. You don't need to be alone to feel abandoned.

The wilderness begins the moment the life you built can no longer sustain the weight of who you are becoming.

For years, I thought the wilderness was punishment, a consequence for my failures, a sign that God was disappointed in me, a place where I had to prove myself worthy again. But the wilderness is not where God sends the rejected. It is where He forms the chosen.

The wilderness strips away the illusions you used to survive. It exposes the habits you hid behind. It reveals the desires you never confronted. It forces you to face the truth without the distractions that once numbed you.

In the wilderness, there is no applause. No validation. No shortcuts. No noise to drown out the voice you've been avoiding.

Just you. And God. And the parts of yourself you've been running from.

The wilderness is uncomfortable because it is honest. It reveals the gap between who you pretend to be and who you actually are. It reveals the wounds you never healed. It reveals the idols you never admitted you worshipped.

But the wilderness is also where transformation begins.

It is where God breaks the patterns that broke you. It is where He confronts the lies you believed about yourself. It is where He teaches you dependence, not the fragile dependence of desperation, but the steady dependence of trust.

The wilderness is not a detour. It is the path.

Every person who has ever walked the narrow road has walked through the wilderness first. Not because God delights in your struggle, but because He refuses to let you carry the weight of your old life into your new one.

The wilderness is where the old you dies. Not instantly. Not dramatically. But slowly, through surrender, through honesty, through the quiet realization that you cannot save yourself.

And in that dying, something new begins to grow.

A new identity. A new strength. A new clarity. A new hunger for the God you once ignored.

The wilderness is not the end of your story. It is the beginning of your becoming.

It is where God prepares you for the life you were always meant to live, a life not built on illusion, but on truth. A life not built on performance, but on purpose. A life not built on self-reliance, but on surrender.

The wilderness is not a place to fear. It is a place to be found.

Because in the wilderness, God is not distant. He is near. He is present. He is shaping you with a precision you cannot yet understand.

And when you finally emerge, not rushed, not half healed, not pretending, you will realize that the wilderness was not where you were abandoned.

It was where you were remade.

PART II — FORMATION: THE INNER WORK OF GOD

Chapter 4

The Illusion of Control

Control is the most seductive lie a person can believe. It feels like strength. It feels like intelligence. It feels like maturity. But in reality, control is nothing more than a costume we wear to hide our fear of surrender.

For years, I lived inside that illusion. I thought discipline was control. I thought planning was control. I thought emotional detachment was control. I thought the ability to endure chaos without flinching meant I had mastered myself.

But control is not mastery. Control is fear dressed as competence.

The wide road teaches you that you can build your own destiny if you just push hard enough, grind long enough, and refuse to break. It teaches you that you can shape outcomes through sheer will. It teaches you that you can protect yourself from disappointment by refusing to need anything or anyone.

But the truth is simpler and far more uncomfortable:

You cannot control what you were never meant to carry.

I tried to control my image. I tried to control my relationships. I tried to control my emotions. I tried to control my future. I even tried to control God, not consciously, but through the quiet expectation that He should bless the life I built without Him.

Control is a prison disguised as freedom. It keeps you busy. It keeps you proud. It keeps you isolated. And it keeps you from ever confronting the truth that you are not the center of your own story.

The illusion of control is powerful because it works, until it doesn't. It holds your life together, until it cracks. It gives you confidence, until it collapses under the weight of reality.

And when it collapses, it doesn't fall gently. It shatters.

For me, the shattering came slowly at first, small fractures in the armor I wore. Moments where my strength wasn't enough. Moments where my plans failed. Moments where the people I depended on couldn't carry what I placed on them. Moments where my own heart betrayed me.

Then came the breaking point, the moment where the illusion finally tore open and I saw myself clearly:

A man exhausted from trying to be his own god.

The illusion of control doesn't die quietly. It dies in the moment you realize that surrender is not weakness, it's the only doorway to peace.

When I finally let go, I didn't feel powerful. I didn't feel enlightened. I didn't feel victorious.

I felt relieved.

Relieved that I no longer had to pretend. Relieved that I no longer had to hold everything together. Relieved that I could finally admit I was not in control, and never had been.

The narrow road begins where the illusion of control ends. Not because God wants to take power from you, but because He wants to give you a life that isn't built on fear.

Control is a burden. Surrender is a release. And the moment I stopped gripping my life with white knuckled desperation was the moment I finally felt free.

Chapter 5

The Weight of Meaning

Meaning is not something you stumble into. It is not handed to you by circumstance or inherited from the people who raised you. Meaning is discovered the moment you realize that everything you built on your own terms is too light to carry the weight of your existence.

For most of my life, I treated meaning like a personal project, something I could engineer through achievement, discipline, or reputation. If I worked hard enough, if I stayed sharp enough, if I kept my emotions locked behind steel doors, then surely my life would add up to something.

But meaning is not the sum of your accomplishments. It is the truth that remains when your accomplishments fail to satisfy you.

The wide road teaches you to chase significance through noise, through validation, through status, through the illusion that being seen is the same as being known. But the more you chase meaning through external things, the more hollow you become internally.

I learned this the hard way.

There came a point where everything I had built, the persona, the discipline, the image of strength, felt like a costume I couldn't take off. People saw the armor, but they never saw the man underneath it. And the longer I wore it, the more I forgot who I actually was.

Meaning cannot be found in admiration, performance, or applause. It isn't born from how others see you, but from the truth God reveals about who you are.

But truth is heavy. It confronts you. It exposes the parts of you that you've spent years hiding. It forces you to admit that the life you built without God was not a life at all, just a performance with no audience and no purpose.

The weight of meaning is not the weight of pressure. It is the weight of reality. It is the moment you realize that your soul was not designed to orbit around your own desires.

Meaning is not discovered in the pursuit of self, but in the surrender of self.

When I finally stopped trying to manufacture my own significance, I discovered something I had never experienced before:

Peace.

Not the fragile peace that comes from temporary stability. Not the shallow peace that comes from distraction. But the deep, immovable peace that comes from knowing your life is anchored to something eternal.

Meaning is not found in what you achieve. It is found in who you become when you stop running from the truth.

And the truth is this:

You were made for more than survival. You were made for more than performance. You were made for God, and nothing else will ever satisfy you.

The weight of meaning is not a burden. It is a foundation. And once you stand on it, the storms of life no longer have the power to define you.

Chapter 6

The Echoes of Eden

There is a memory inside every human being that no experience on earth can fully explain. A longing that feels older than our childhood. A hunger that no achievement, relationship, or pleasure can satisfy. A homesickness for a place we've never visited but somehow remember.

That memory is Eden.

Not the garden itself, but the echo of what humanity once was, whole, unbroken, unafraid, and in perfect communion with God. Even if you don't know the story, your soul does. It remembers what it was made for.

And that memory haunts us.

It shows up in our restlessness. In our dissatisfaction. In the way nothing ever feels like enough. In the way we chase meaning through noise, hoping something will finally silence the ache inside us.

But the ache is not a flaw. It is a compass.

The echoes of Eden are the reminders that we were not designed for the world we're trying to survive. We were designed for a world without shame, without fear, without the constant pressure to prove ourselves. We were designed for a world where identity wasn't earned, it was given.

But somewhere along the way, we traded that world for one we thought we could control.

The wide road is built on that trade. It promises freedom but delivers bondage. It promises fulfillment but delivers addiction. It promises identity but delivers confusion. It promises life but delivers exhaustion.

And yet, even in the middle of that exhaustion, the echoes remain.

They whisper in the quiet moments, the moments when the distractions fade and the truth rises to the surface. They whisper when the things we thought would satisfy us leave us emptier than before. They whisper when we realize that the life we built is too small for the soul we carry.

The echoes of Eden are not nostalgia. They are revelation.

They reveal that the deepest parts of us are not shaped by our failures, our trauma, or our desires, but by the fingerprints of the One who made us. They reveal that our longing for meaning is not a psychological glitch but a spiritual memory. They reveal that the ache we feel is not a sign that something is wrong with us, but that something is missing from us.

And that something is God.

The narrow road does not begin with discipline or morality. It begins with honesty, the honesty to admit that the life we built apart from God cannot satisfy the soul He created.

The echoes of Eden are not meant to shame us. They are meant to guide us home.

They remind us that we were made for communion, not isolation. For truth, not illusion. For purpose, not performance. For God, not ourselves.

And the moment we stop running from that truth is the moment the narrow road becomes visible, not as a restriction, but as a return.

A return to the life we were always meant to live. A return to the identity we lost. A return to the God we abandoned but who never abandoned us.

The echoes of Eden are not faint. They are persistent. They are patient. They are merciful.

And if you listen closely, you will hear them calling you, not backward, but forward. Not into the past, but into restoration. Not into nostalgia, but into redemption.

Eden is not behind us. It is ahead of us. And the narrow road is the path that leads there.

Chapter 7

The Crossroads of Choice

Every life reaches a point where the road splits. Not in the dramatic way movies portray it, no thunder, no spotlight, no booming voice from the sky. The crossroads comes quietly. It comes in the stillness after you've exhausted every excuse. It comes when the life you've been living can no longer carry the weight of who you are becoming.

The crossroads is not about opportunity. It is about honesty.

It is the moment you realize that continuing on the wide road will cost you more than you are willing to lose. It is the moment you understand that the narrow road will require more than you are willing to give. And you stand there, suspended between who you were and who you could be.

Choice is the most sacred power God gave humanity. Not the power to control outcomes, that illusion died long ago, but the power to surrender. The power to turn. The power to walk away from the life that is killing you.

The crossroads exposes your loyalties. It reveals what you truly worship. It reveals what you fear losing. It reveals what you trust more than God.

For me, the crossroads was not a single moment. It was a series of moments, small, piercing confrontations with truth. Moments where God asked me questions I didn't want to answer:

"Is this who you want to be?" "Is this the life you want to die with?" "Is this the road you want to call home?"

The crossroads is not about choosing between good and evil. It is about choosing between truth and illusion. Between surrender and self-preservation. Between the life God offers and the life you built to protect your wounds.

The wide road is familiar. It is predictable. It is comfortable in its misery. It requires nothing from you except the willingness to stay asleep.

The narrow road is different. It demands awakening. It demands courage. It demands the death of the version of yourself that survived through pride, fear, and self-reliance.

The crossroads is where you decide which version of yourself will live.

And the truth is this: You cannot walk the narrow road with the same heart that walked the wide one.

Something has to break. Something has to be surrendered. Something has to be left behind.

For me, it was the illusion that I could save myself. The illusion that I could heal without God. The illusion that I could carry my own shame and still call it strength.

The crossroads is not a test. It is an invitation. An invitation to step into the life you were created for, not the life you settled for.

But every invitation requires a response.

You cannot stand at the crossroads forever. Indecision is a decision. Silence is a direction. Delay is a path.

Eventually, you must choose.

And when you finally take that first step onto the narrow road, you realize something profound:

The crossroads was never about choosing a path. It was about choosing a Master.

The wide road belongs to you, and it will destroy you. The narrow road belongs to God, and it will save you.

The crossroads is where you decide whose hands your life will rest in.

And the moment you choose Him, the road, though narrow, becomes clear.

Chapter 8

The Long Obedience

Obedience is not glamorous. It is not dramatic. It is not the kind of thing people applaud or post about. Obedience is quiet. Obedience is repetitive. Obedience is the slow, steady choice to walk in the same direction even when your emotions, your desires, and your circumstances try to pull you off the path.

The narrow road is not walked through passion. It is walked through perseverance.

For years, I thought transformation happened in moments, breakthroughs, revelations, emotional encounters. But real transformation is not built on moments. It is built on habits. On the daily decision to choose truth over comfort, surrender over pride, discipline over impulse.

The long obedience is where faith becomes more than belief. It becomes a lifestyle.

Obedience is not about perfection. It is about direction. It is the willingness to keep moving forward even when you stumble, even when you fail, even when you feel unworthy of the road you're on.

The wide road is easy because it requires nothing from you. The narrow road is difficult because it requires everything, not all at once, but piece by piece, day by day, choice by choice.

Obedience is the slow death of the old self. Not the dramatic kind of death, but the quiet kind, the kind that happens when you choose patience instead of anger, humility instead of pride, forgiveness instead of bitterness, truth instead of convenience.

Every act of obedience is a small surrender. And every surrender makes room for God to reshape you.

The long obedience is not about earning God's approval. It is about aligning your life with the truth of who He is. It is about trusting that His way is better even when it feels harder. It is about believing that the narrow road leads somewhere worth going.

There were days when obedience felt natural, when clarity was strong and conviction was sharp. But there were also days when obedience felt impossible, when my emotions were louder than my faith, when my past tried to reclaim me, when the old patterns whispered promises of comfort.

Those were the days that mattered most.

Obedience is not proven in your strength. It is proven in your weakness, in the moments when you choose God even when everything in you wants to choose yourself.

The long obedience is not a sprint. It is a pilgrimage. A journey that reshapes you slowly, intentionally, deeply.

And somewhere along that journey, you begin to realize something profound:

Obedience is not a burden. It is freedom.

Freedom from the lies that once controlled you. Freedom from the impulses that once defined you. Freedom from the identity you built out of fear and survival.

Obedience is the path back to yourself, not the self you created, but the self-God intended.

The long obedience is not easy. But it is worth it. Because every step you take on the narrow road is a step toward becoming the person you were always meant to be.

PART III — CALLING: THE MAN GOD IS RAISING UP

Chapter 9

The Narrow Road: Discipline, Scripture, And the Fight Within

There are parts of my story that don't show up on the surface. People see the man I'm becoming, but they don't always see the fight it took to get here, the internal war, the quiet battles, the moments where I had to choose between who I was and who God was calling me to be. The narrow road isn't just a path; it's a discipline. It's a decision you make every day, sometimes every hour.

Pressure has a way of revealing what you really believe. When life tightens around you, when tension rises like a storm, when everything feels like it's closing in, you learn quickly whether your faith is built on sand or stone. I've had days where the pressure felt unbearable, where the air itself felt heavy, where my thoughts were louder than my prayers. But even then, I knew something deeper, something truer.

God was still in control. He was the One who commanded the wind, the One who steadied the air, the One who kept me from collapsing under the weight of my own thoughts. I didn't always feel strong, but I felt held. And sometimes, that's the only strength you need.

But discipline, that's a different story. Discipline isn't emotional. It isn't dramatic. It isn't loud. Discipline is quiet, steady, and often uncomfortable. It's choosing Scripture when your mind wants distraction. It's choosing prayer when your flesh wants escape. It's choosing truth when lies feel easier to swallow.

There were days I held back from reading the Word. Not because I didn't believe it, but because I knew it would cut me. Scripture doesn't just comfort; it confronts. It exposes motives, reveals wounds, and demands honesty. And sometimes, I wasn't ready to face myself. I wasn't ready to let God speak into the parts of me I kept hidden.

But withholding Scripture from myself was a quiet betrayal. Not against God, He doesn't lose anything when I avoid His Word. It was a betrayal against my own soul. A self-inflicted wound. A slow, silent killer.

Every time I avoided the Word, I felt it. A chill down my spine. A sense of drifting. A reminder that the battle wasn't out there, it was in me.

Temptation didn't disappear just because I started praying. It changed shape. It dressed itself in old glamour, old habits, old desires. It came wrapped in nostalgia, in memories that lied about how good things used to be. Temptation doesn't show you the consequences; it shows you the highlight reel. It shows you the smile, not the aftermath. It shows you the thrill, not the wreckage.

And I felt the pull. Not because I wanted to go back, but because the flesh remembers what the spirit has forgotten. The world knows how to whisper. The past knows how to call your name. The old life knows how to make itself look beautiful again.

But every time I felt that rise inside me, that urge to escape, to numb, to drift, I realized something important:

It wasn't temptation calling me back.

It was God reminding me how much I needed Him.

The narrow road isn't about perfection. It's about dependence. It's about choosing God when everything in you wants to choose something else. It's about letting Scripture cut you so it can heal you. It's about letting prayer steady you when the world shakes. It's about walking forward even when the past tries to drag you back.

This chapter of my life wasn't glamorous. It wasn't dramatic. It wasn't something people would applaud. But it was real. And it was necessary.

Because before you can walk the narrow road, you have to learn how to fight the battles inside yourself.

Chapter 10

Cultural Lament: The World on Fire

There came a point in my walk where the battle wasn't just inside me anymore. It was around me, in the streets, in the culture, in the conversations people had without thinking, in the choices they made without blinking. I started seeing the world differently, not because the world changed, but because I did. When God opens your eyes, you can't unsee what's broken.

This is my new M.O., not the teenage kind, not the dramatic kind, but the spiritual kind. It's the ache of a man who feels too much, sees too much, and can't pretend everything is fine. It's the weight of carrying emotions that don't fit neatly into sentences. It's the Spirit guiding the pen, pulling truth out of me whether I want to write it or not.

The world feels twisted. Not just troubled, twisted. Like two armies gathering on opposite sides of a valley, preparing for a final clash. You can feel it in the air, in the tension between people, in the way society moves with a kind of reckless confidence, unaware of the cliff it's sprinting toward.

Church bells ring, but instead of peace, they stir something else. Anger. Restlessness. A sense that people are tired of God before they've ever truly met Him. The sound that once called people to worship now irritates the ears of a generation that wants freedom without truth, pleasure without consequence, spirituality without submission.

It reminds me of Jerusalem, not the holy city, but the crowd. The crowd that chose Barabbas over the God of heaven. The crowd that preferred a criminal to a Savior. The crowd that shouted for the release of a man who took life, while demanding the death of the One who came to give it.

And I look around today and see the same spirit. People choosing what destroys them. People cheering for what kills them. People rejecting the only One who can save them.

And here I am, some hood kid trying to make sense of the riddles and the madness. I'm not a scholar. I'm not a theologian. I'm not a philosopher. I'm just a man who lived enough life to recognize when the world is burning.

But the part that breaks me the most isn't the culture. It's the children.

There's a boy named Belly with no one in his corner. No friends. No family. No safety net. Just a small life trying to survive in a world that doesn't care if he makes it to tomorrow.

And there's a girl named Susie carrying fear no child should ever know. Fear that creeps into her room at night. Fear that steals her innocence. Fear that no one sees because everyone is too busy pretending everything is fine.

These are the ones who haunt me. Not the politicians. Not the celebrities. Not the influencers. The children. The forgotten. The ones who suffer quietly while the world argues loudly.

I carry them in my prayers. I carry them in my writing. I carry them in the way I see the world, not as a battlefield of ideas, but as a place where real people bleed, break, and disappear without anyone noticing.

This chapter of my life wasn't about judgment. It was about grief. A grief that comes from seeing the world clearly for the first time. A grief that pushes me to intercede, to speak, to write, to warn, to hope.

Because even though the world is on fire, I believe God still walks through the flames. And if He hasn't given up on us, then neither will I.

Chapter 11

Identity And Calling: Who I Am and Whose I Am

There's a moment in every man's life when he realizes he can't walk alone. For some, that moment comes early. For others, it comes late. For me, it came after I had already tried to carry too much on my own. I wasn't built for isolation, but I lived like I was. I moved through life with a kind of stubborn independence, convinced that needing help made me weak. I didn't understand that walking alone wasn't strength, it was survival. And survival isn't the same as living.

I've known locked doors. I've known dead ends. I've known the feeling of standing at a crossroads with nowhere left to turn. Those moments taught me something I couldn't have learned any other way: the wide road is crowded for a reason. It's easy. It's loud. It's full of distractions and shortcuts and people who don't want to think about eternity.

But the narrow road, that's different. It's quiet. It's demanding. It's lonely at times. And it requires a kind of honesty most people spend their whole lives avoiding.

The truth is simple:

You choose your path.

No one chooses it for you.

I had to learn that the hard way. I had to learn that eternity isn't something you drift into. You don't stumble into righteousness. You don't accidentally become disciplined. You don't wake up one day and find yourself holy by coincidence. The narrow road requires intention. It requires surrender. It requires a willingness to walk away from the noise, even when the noise feels familiar.

My eyes stay fixed on the sparrow's Keeper. That's not just a poetic line, it's a confession. It's me admitting that I need Someone watching over me, Someone guiding me, Someone who sees what I don't. The sparrow doesn't worry about tomorrow because it knows who holds it. I'm learning to live the same way.

But the world doesn't stop calling just because you've chosen a different path. Another bottle can still call your name. Another memory can still whisper. Another escape can still offer an encore.

For me, it was the Blue Note Jazz Club, not the place itself, but what it represented. The temptation to drift. The temptation to numb. The temptation to return to the familiar rhythm of old habits. The temptation to drown the quiet voice of conviction with something louder.

But I've learned something about temptation:

It doesn't disappear.

It just loses its authority when you stop bowing to it.

Let the masses drift where the noise is loud. Let them chase the wide road if they want to. Let them choose what's easy.

I'll take the route where only a few are willing to go. Not because I'm better. Not because I'm stronger. But because I've seen what the wide road leads to, and I refuse to go back.

This chapter of my life isn't about pride. It's about clarity. It's about knowing who I am, and more importantly, knowing whose I am.

I belong to the One who kept me alive when I didn't care if I lived. I belong to the One who steadied me when everything shook. I belong to the One who called me out of the crowd and onto the narrow road. I belong to the One who watches the sparrow, and watches me.

Identity isn't something you find. It's something God reveals. And calling isn't something you earn. It's something you answer.

I'm answering mine, one step at a time, on the road where only a few go.

Chapter 12

The Anthem of Freedom: Praise Instead of Mourning

Freedom didn't arrive quietly in my life. It didn't slip in through the back door or whisper its way into my decisions. It came like a breaking, a tearing, a moment where everything I thought I needed collapsed, and everything I truly needed stood waiting in the wreckage. I didn't walk into freedom with confidence. I stumbled into it with relief.

Let judgment fall on the life I left behind. I don't say that with bitterness. I say it with honesty. The man I used to be needed to die. Not physically, spiritually. Emotionally. Habitually. The version of me that lived for escape, for numbness, for survival, for the approval of people who didn't care if I lived or died, that man had to go.

I was a wanderer once. Both arms bound. Both eyes blind. Both feet walking toward a cliff I didn't see. I didn't realize how close I came to losing everything, not just my future, but my soul. There were moments when destruction felt like the only ending I was headed toward. But God intervened in ways I didn't recognize until much later.

Thank God I never boarded that doomed ship. There were paths I almost took, decisions I almost made, people I almost followed, addictions I almost surrendered to. Any one of them could have ended me. But grace has a way of interrupting a man's downfall. Mercy has a way of pulling you back from the edge even when you don't know you're standing on it.

This is my anthem now, not a song of mourning, but a song of freedom.

Let the spirit rise. Let the soul dance. Let the joy shake loose every last restraint. If I don't praise, the pressure inside me will turn to chaos. Praise isn't a performance for me, it's survival. It's the release valve that keeps my heart from exploding under the weight of everything I've lived through.

I think of David in Jerusalem, dancing with no shame, no hesitation, no concern for who was watching. He wasn't performing. He was celebrating the God who saved him from lions, giants, enemies, and himself.

I understand that now. I understand what it means to praise like a man who survived something he shouldn't have. I understand what it means to lift my hands not because life is perfect, but because God is faithful.

Whose son am I? Not the son of my past. Not the son of my mistakes. Not the son of the streets that tried to claim me. I am the son of the One who rode a donkey through crowded streets, the King who chose humility over spectacle, the Savior who chose a cross over a throne, the Shepherd who chose me when I wasn't choosing Him.

Let the women lift their voices, not in mourning, but in celebration. Let the pastor proclaim freedom from every corner of the block. Let the sound of redemption echo through the neighborhoods that once echoed with sirens and sorrow.

As for the delinquents who used to haunt these streets, you won't hear their names in the missing reports. Grace found them first. Mercy reached them before the grave did. God rewrote their stories the same way He rewrote mine.

This chapter of my life isn't about pretending everything is perfect. It's about acknowledging that everything is redeemed. It's about celebrating the

God who broke my chains, rewrote my ending, and turned my mourning into a song.

> Freedom isn't quiet.
>
> Freedom isn't polite.
>
> Freedom isn't subtle.
>
> Freedom is loud.
>
> Freedom is holy.
>
> Freedom is mine.

BENEDICTION: THE MAN WHO WALKS FORWARD

I stand here now as a man shaped by everything I've lived through, not defined by it, not chained to it, but shaped by it. There's a difference. Some people carry their past like a sentence. I carry mine like a testimony. I don't hide where I came from, but I don't bow to it either. God didn't bring me this far to make me a prisoner of my own history.

The storms didn't break me. They revealed me. They showed me what was fragile, what was false, what was temporary. They stripped away the illusions I built around myself, the toughness, the pride, the independence, the masks I wore to survive. Storms don't ask for permission. They expose whatever isn't anchored. And I learned quickly that the only anchor strong enough to hold me was God Himself.

Temptations didn't claim me. Not because I was strong, but because God was patient. There were moments when I felt the old life tug at me, the familiar escapes, the old habits, the voices that once had authority over my decisions. But every time I felt myself slipping, God reminded me who I was becoming. He didn't shame me. He didn't threaten me. He simply held me steady until I could stand again.

The world didn't swallow me. It tried. It offered me shortcuts, distractions, illusions of success, illusions of freedom. It tried to convince me that the wide road was easier, safer, more comfortable. But comfort is a liar. Ease is a trap. The world doesn't care about your soul, it only cares that you stay asleep.

I'm awake now. And once you're awake, you can't go back to sleep.

I walk forward with gratitude, not the shallow kind, not the polite kind, but the kind that comes from knowing you should've been dead, lost, or forgotten, but you're still here. Gratitude that comes from knowing God intervened in ways you didn't deserve. Gratitude that comes from seeing how far you've come and realizing you didn't walk a single step alone.

I walk forward with discipline, not because I enjoy it, but because I need it. Discipline is the guardrail that keeps me on the narrow road. It's the structure that protects the freedom God gave me. It's the daily choice to open Scripture, to pray, to stay honest, to stay humble, to stay awake.

I walk forward with a heart that knows who carried me. I don't pretend I made it here by intelligence, strength, or willpower. I made it here because God refused to let me go. He carried me through confusion, through temptation, through cultural chaos, through internal battles, through the ruins of my old life. And He's still carrying me, not because I'm weak, but because I'm His.

This is my testimony. Not a story of perfection, but a story of pursuit. Not a story of a man who found God, but a story of a God who found a man. Not a story of escape, but a story of redemption.

This is my offering. Every word, every chapter, every confession, every reflection, it's all an altar. Not to my strength, but to His mercy. Not to my wisdom, but to His patience. Not to my journey, but to His faithfulness.

This is my freedom song. A song sung by a man who knows what chains feel like. A song sung by a man who knows what grace feels like. A song sung by a man who refuses to go back to the life that almost destroyed him.

I choose the narrow road every time. Not because it's easy. Not because it's popular. But because it's the only road that leads to life.

And I walk it with confidence, not in myself, but in the God who walks it with me

EPILOGUE

THE QUIET AFTER THE FIRE

There's a silence that comes after transformation. Not the silence of emptiness, but the silence of completion, the kind that settles over a man when he realizes he survived what was meant to destroy him. I've lived through storms, temptations, cultural chaos, internal battles, and the slow rebuilding of a life I once thought was beyond repair. And now, standing on the other side, the world feels different.

Not easier.

Not softer.

Just clearer.

I used to think the goal was to escape my past. Now I understand the goal was to understand it, to see it for what it was, to learn from it, to let God use it as raw material for something new. My past isn't a chain anymore. It's a testimony. It's a reminder of where I've been and a marker of how far God has brought me.

I don't pretend to have everything figured out. I don't pretend to be perfect. I don't pretend to be above the struggles that shaped me. But I'm not who I was. And I'm not going back.

The narrow road is still narrow. The world is still loud. Temptation still whispers. But I walk differently now, not with fear, but with awareness. Not with pride, but with gratitude. Not with confusion, but with clarity.

I know who carries me.

I know who keeps me.

I know who calls me forward.

And I know this:

God didn't save me so I could stay silent.

He didn't rebuild me so I could hide.

He didn't free me so I could blend in.

My life is an offering now, not a perfect one, but a willing one.

If someone reads these pages and sees themselves in my story, if someone feels less alone, if someone finds the courage to pray again, if someone chooses the narrow road because they saw what God did in me, then every chapter was worth writing.

This isn't the end of my story. It's the end of this book, but not the end of the work God is doing in me.

I walk forward with open hands, steady steps, and a heart that knows the One who began a good work in me will finish it.

And I'm ready for whatever comes next.

ACKNOWLEDGMENTS

To those who walked beside me, even when I didn't know how to walk beside myself.

To the people who saw the cracks before I admitted they were there. To the ones who prayed when I was too stubborn to ask for help. To the ones who spoke truth when I only wanted comfort. To the ones who stayed when my life was a storm and my heart was a battlefield.

You were instruments of mercy long before I recognized it.

To the voices that challenged me, sharpened me, and refused to let me settle for the version of myself that was slowly destroying me, thank you. Your honesty was a lifeline. Your patience was a mirror. Your presence was a reminder that God often sends people before He sends answers.

To those who offered correction without condemnation, guidance without control, and love without conditions, you helped me see the narrow road when all I could see was the wreckage of the wide one.

To the ones who didn't give up on me when I was ready to give up on myself, your faith carried me farther than my strength ever could.

And to the quiet supporters, the ones who never asked for recognition, the ones who encouraged from the background, the ones who believed in the work even before it had a name, this book carries your fingerprints.

Finally, to the God who never abandoned me, even when I abandoned Him, every page is a testimony of Your patience, Your pursuit, and Your unrelenting grace.

Thank you for the wilderness. Thank you for the crossroads. Thank you for the narrow road.

AUTHOR'S NOTE

This book was born in silence and struggle. Not the kind of struggle people see, but the kind that lives beneath the surface, the kind that shapes you quietly, the kind that forces you to confront the truth you've avoided for years.

I did not write these chapters from a place of mastery. I wrote them from a place of becoming. Every page carries the weight of lessons learned the hard way, through failure, through surrender, through the slow dismantling of the illusions I once called strength.

If these words feel honest, it is because they were written in honesty. If they feel heavy, it is because they were forged in the places where God confronted me. If they feel hopeful, it is because grace has a way of finding you even when you're not looking for it.

I did not set out to write a book. I set out to survive. And somewhere along the way, survival turned into transformation.

My hope is not that you admire these pages, but that you recognize yourself in them. That you see your own wilderness, your own crossroads, your own echoes of Eden. That you realize you are not alone in the tension between who you were and who you are becoming.

The narrow road is not easy. But it is real. And it is worth it.

If this book does anything, let it be this: Let it remind you that God is patient. That He is present. That He is not intimidated by your brokenness or exhausted by your process. That He is still calling you, not to perfection, but to Himself.

Thank you for walking these pages with me. Thank you for letting my story speak into yours. And thank you for choosing, even now, to keep walking the narrow road.

www.ingramcontent.com/pod-product-compliance
Lightning Source LLC
LaVergne TN
LVHW041645070526
838199LV00053B/3567